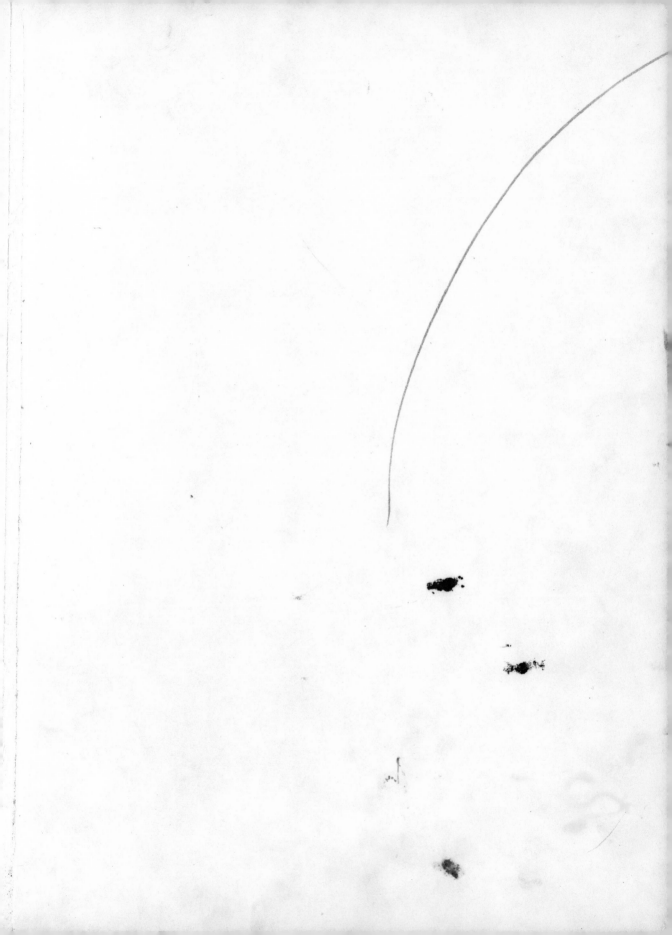

JOANNA COLE

Saber-Toothed Tiger

AND OTHER
ICE AGE MAMMALS

ILLUSTRATED BY LYDIA ROSIER

William Morrow & Company
New York 1977

To Amanda and Hannah Treitel

Library of Congress Cataloging in Publication Data

Cole, Joanna.
    Saber-toothed tiger and other ice age mammals.

    SUMMARY: Describes such Ice Age mammals as
the saber-toothed tiger, mastodon, and cave bear.
    1. Smilodon—Juvenile literature.   2. Mammals,
Fossil—Juvenile literature.   3. Paleontology—
Pleistocene—Juvenile literature.
[1. Mammals, Fossil.   2. Paleontology]
I. Rosier, Lydia.   II. Title.
QE882.C15C64   569   77-9957
ISBN 0-688-22120-3
ISBN 0-688-32120-8 lib. bdg.

About three million years ago,
something strange happened to the earth.
It began to get colder and colder.
The ice caps in the north started to grow.
They moved south over the earth.
The Great Ice Age was beginning.

After thousands of years
much of the earth was covered with thick sheets of ice.
These sheets were called glaciers.

Most animals could not live near the freezing glaciers.
The animals moved south.

4

During the Ice Age,
the great walls of ice moved south four times.
And four times they melted and went back.
When the glaciers melted,
the earth was as warm as it is now.
Then the animals moved north again.

The Ice Age lasted for a very long time.
It lasted until ten thousand years ago.

The time of the dinosaurs was gone.
They had died out long before.
No dinosaur lived during the Ice Age.
But other kinds of animals had come into being.
They were warm-blooded, and they had fur or hair.
These new animals were called mammals.

People are mammals too.
There were people during the Ice Age.
Prehistoric human beings lived during the Ice Age.

The fiercest Ice Age mammal was a big cat
called the saber-toothed tiger.
It was as big as a lion.
But it was heavier and stronger than a lion.
It had long, sharp fangs in its upper jaw.

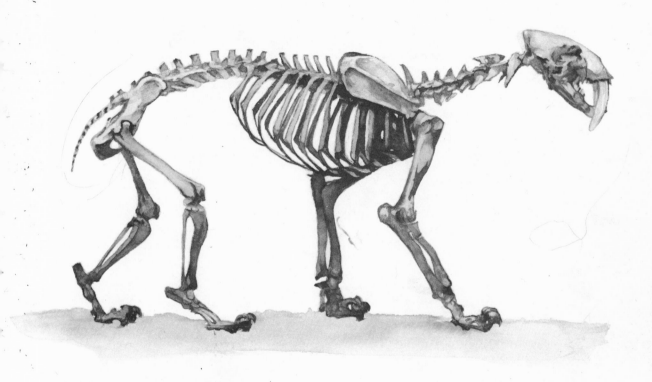

No one has ever seen a live sabertooth.
All of them died out long ago.
But the bones of saber-toothed tigers have been found.
Scientists can tell what sabertooths
were like from the bones.

9

Saber-toothed tigers were meat eaters.
They hunted other animals for food.

Saber-toothed cats could not run fast.
But they were strong.
They could kill large, slow animals.

A sabertooth did not bite an animal.
Instead of biting, it used its fangs to stab the animal.
The sabertooth's lower jaw could open very wide.
Then the fangs on the upper jaw were free to stab.

A saber-toothed tiger was strong enough
to kill a woolly mammoth.
This animal was a prehistoric elephant.
It was the size of a modern elephant.

The woolly mammoth lived near the glaciers.
It had a coat of shaggy red fur.
Under its skin, it had a thick layer of fat.
On its head and shoulders were humps of fat
like a camel's humps.
Its woolly coat and its fat
helped keep the mammoth warm.

A mammoth's tusks curved in.
They formed a kind of snowplow.
The mammoth used its tusks to push snow away.
Then it ate the grass that was under the snow.

When a saber-toothed tiger hunted a woolly mammoth,
it probably chose a small, weak one.
If a sabertooth saw a mammoth
lagging behind the rest of the herd,
it leaped on the mammoth's back.
It stabbed the mammoth many times with its fangs.
It held on with its strong claws.
14 The mammoth could not shake off the sabertooth.

Prehistoric men hunted the woolly mammoth too.
They set fires and stampeded the mammoths
over the edge of a cliff.
Then the hunters killed them with spears.

People have found paintings of woolly mammoths
on the walls of caves.
These paintings were made by prehistoric human beings
thousands of years ago during the Ice Age.
They are still in the caves for us to see today.

15

Scientists have found the bodies of woolly mammoths.
In Siberia there are places
where the ground is always frozen.
There scientists found a woolly mammoth.
It had been frozen solid
for more than thirty thousand years!

The scientists dug up the mammoth.
It looked just as it looked when it died.
There were thirty pounds of food still in its stomach.
This is what the mammoth had eaten:
grass, moss, seeds, flowers,
and the branches of pine trees.

In Alaska another woolly mammoth
was found in the frozen ground.
It was a baby mammoth.
It was only one year old when it died.

There were other kinds of prehistoric elephants.
The biggest was called an emperor mammoth.
This name means king of the mammoths.
18   The emperor mammoth did not have heavy fur.

Another elephant was the mastodon.
It had long red fur and big tusks.
It looked different from the woolly mammoth.
Its head was longer, and it did not have humps.

Woolly mammoths and mastodons
were not the only animals with heavy fur.
The woolly rhinoceros had thick, dark fur
and long bristles.
It had two horns. One was long and one was short.
Like modern rhinos, the woolly rhino was a plant eater.
It ate the leaves of trees and bushes.

If a saber-toothed tiger attacked,
the woolly rhino would charge with its sharp horns.

The cave bear looked fierce,
but it was really a peaceful animal.
It was large, though—
about the size of a modern grizzly bear.
Like the bears of today,
cave bears went into a deep sleep in the winter.
This sleep is called hibernation.

Scientists have found caves that the bears used.
One cave was filled with *thousands* of bear skeletons!

People used to think that prehistoric human beings
hunted the bears and put the bones in the cave.
But today scientists believe the bears died in their sleep.
Sick bears died while they were hibernating.
Only a few bears died every year.
But the bears used the cave for thousands of years.
That is why there were so many skeletons all in one cave.

Many mammals of the Ice Age were giants.
This animal is a giant ground sloth.
Its relatives of today are tree sloths.
They are small, sleepy animals
that hang from the branches of trees.
They are only about two or three feet long.

But the giant ground sloth was twenty feet tall.
It was tall enough to look over the roof of a house.
It weighed five tons,
which is as heavy as a modern elephant.

Most of the time,
giant ground sloths led a peaceful life.
They sat on their haunches
and ate leaves from the treetops.
Today baby tree sloths hang onto their mothers' fur.
Maybe the babies of giant ground sloths
traveled this way too.

The giant ground sloth was a slow animal.
It walked in an awkward way
on the sides of its feet.
To protect itself from enemies,
it had long claws on its front feet.

If a sabertooth came near,
the sloth would sit up and swing its heavy front feet.

One giant mammal had armor to protect it from enemies.
It was the giant armadillo.
Today armadillos are small animals about three feet long.
But the giant armadillo of the Ice Age
was fourteen feet long and six feet high—
about the size of a minibus.

Its body was covered with a hard, bony plate
like a turtle's shell.
Even its tail was covered with bony rings.

One kind of armadillo had a club on the end of its tail.
The club had sharp spikes.

If an enemy attacked,
this armadillo could swing its tail from side to side.
A saber-toothed tiger could not kill
either of these ancient armadillos.

Another giant was the giant beaver.
It was as big as a bear.

The giant beavers did not build dams
the way modern beavers do.
But they may have eaten the same foods
as modern beavers:
small plants, twigs, and the bark of trees.

30

The great Irish deer was a plant eater too.
It had the biggest antlers any deer has ever had.
They were ten feet across from tip to tip.
They weighed eighty pounds.

Some scientists think that the antlers
were too heavy for the deer.
Some deer may have fallen over
when they leaned down to drink!

31

Many plant-eating animals ran in herds.
Where the United States is today,
there were herds of horses, camels,
giant bison, or buffaloes,
and tiny antelopes only two feet tall.

Most of these plant eaters were too quick
for the saber-toothed tiger.
It could not run fast enough to catch them.

Another cat hunted these animals.
It was a giant jaguar.
The giant jaguar had teeth like those
of the cats we know today.
It used its upper and lower teeth
to bite the animals it killed.
It was a biting cat.
It was not a stabbing cat
like the saber-toothed tiger.

The giant jaguar was fast and stealthy.
It hunted fast animals on the open plains.

Prehistoric wolves, called dire wolves,
could kill fast animals too.
They ran together in packs.
They could surround a fast animal and kill it.
They were like the wolves of today.

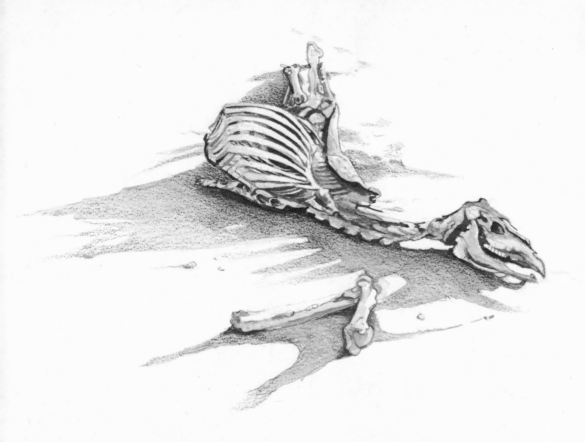

The bones of saber-toothed tigers, dire wolves,
and giant jaguars have been found in the tar pits
of Rancho La Brea in Los Angeles, California.

These deep pools of sticky tar existed in prehistoric times.
When scientists dug up bones from the tar pits,
they found the skeletons of thousands of animals.
For every *one* plant eater, there were *ten* meat eaters.
This find told the scientists what had happened.

When one plant eater got stuck in the tar,
many meat eaters heard its cries.
They came and tried to reach the plant eater.
36   Then they got stuck too.

When it rained, the tar was covered with water.
Then it looked like a lake.
Animals came to drink the water.

First some mastodons came.
They stood at the edge of the water to drink.
They sprayed water with their trunks.

Then a herd of giant bison and some camels came.

A pack of dire wolves watched a small herd of horses.
If a horse strayed away from the herd,
the wolves would attack.

A small ground sloth
came lumbering down to the water.
It waded in and started to drink.
Then it let out a cry. Its feet were stuck in the tar.
The sloth tried to get out.
But the more it tried, the deeper it sank in the tar.

Suddenly a roar sounded.
The other animals turned to look.

A hungry saber-toothed tiger
was looking at the helpless ground sloth.

The sabertooth jumped.
It landed on the ground sloth.
It stabbed the ground sloth with its fangs.

But another hungry cat had heard
the cries of the ground sloth too.
It was a giant jaguar.
The jaguar jumped.
It tried to push the sabertooth off the ground sloth.
It sank its claws into the sabertooth's back.

But the sabertooth shook off the jaguar.
The jaguar fell into the tar.
Now it was stuck too.

When the saber-toothed tiger finished its meal,
it jumped off the ground sloth.
It landed on dry ground.

In the air giant vultures flew in circles.
They swooped down on what was left
of the ground sloth.
The wings of one vulture stuck in the tar.

In a few hours, the victims were gone.
The ground sloth, the jaguar, and the vulture
had all sunk beneath the tar.

This time the sabertooth had been lucky.
But next time it too might lose its life in the tar pits.   45

Most of the Ice Age mammals
died out when the Ice Age ended.

Some scientists think they died
because the earth became too warm.

46

Others think that prehistoric men
caused the animals to become extinct.
Early human hunters may have killed them off.

But no one knows for sure
why the Ice Age mammals died out.

Most scientists believe that someday
the glaciers may move south again.
Then there will be another ice age.

But the fabulous mammals of the Great Ice Age
are gone forever.
We know them only through messages from the past—
their bones, their frozen bodies,
and the cave paintings of prehistoric people.

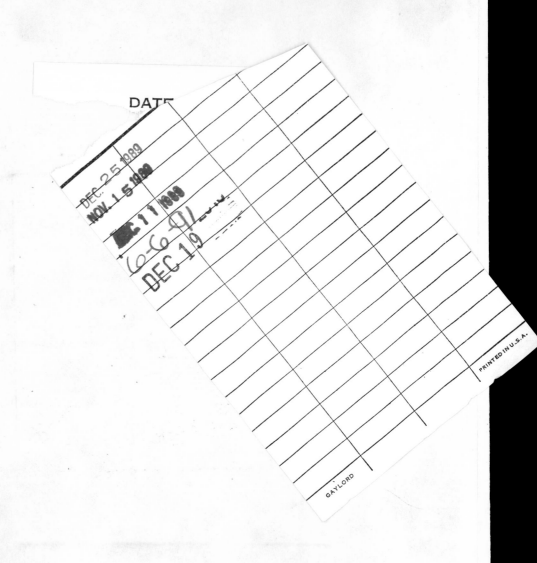